Soulscot *

Poems 1960 – 1973

HARVEY MUDD

* Soulscot: something paid for a soul's requiem . . .

Published by Second Porcupine Press
P.O. Box 548, Santa Fe, New Mexico 87501

Santa Fé, New Mexico

Certain of these poems have previously appeared in the following publications: Black Bear Review; *Childhood II, Mail for Jaime, California Burial, Concerning Destinations, In Boston Common, Spinoza's Dog.* Green River Review; *Easter Sunday, Cordoba.* Twigs; *For Jaime, at Home, The Dice and Sunday.* Southern Poetry Review; *Senator from Carthage.* Loon; *August in Oklahoma.* Stonecloud; *After Venus, Ditch Cleaning, Poem Addressed to my Father, The Expulsion.* Sunstone Review; *For Jaime, in Mexico.*

An Extract from *The Near Sierra* has appeared in *For Neruda, for Chile* (1975) and is reprinted with the permission of Beacon Press.

Drought and *Poem about the Water* will appear in Southwest, A Contemporary Anthology, edited by Karl Kopp, Spring 1977.

This book is dedicated to my teachers, in order of appearance:

Kathleen Clifford
Charlie Nebeker
Hamish Robertson
Frank Butler
David Lavender
Charles Wells
Shervert Frazier
Eugenio Villicana

and especially to Alicia Cahue

*And for invaluable advice and encouragement with this manuscript
the author acknowledges and thanks Jack Parsons, James Levy,
Jean Culpepper, Kathleen Laurent, and Shirley Taylor.*

TABLE OF CONTENTS

Ceremony 15

I "the Warrior Boy named Darkness . . ."
Poise, a Cowboy Poem 19
A Nativity: L.A. 1940 20
Childhood I. 22
1943 27
1944 28

II "Death is Obsessed with me . . ."
Crow's Version 31
For Jaime, in Mexico. 35
Cerberus to the Mole. 36
In the Tropics 37
Death in Mexico 39
Jeremiad 41
Intimations 42
Elegy. 43
Death, Listen. 45

III "I sense the continent diminish . . ."
In Boston Common. 51
On Mount Tamalpais. 52
August in Oklahoma 53
Sky Full of Beasts. 54
The Encantadas. 55
In La Mancha 56
Poem about the Water. 57
Drought. 60

IV "the strike of intellect upon the stone . . ."
Know This. 63
The Holy Man 64
The Dice and Sunday 65
Spinoza's Dog 67
China Always is Near. 68
To a Great Sea Tortoise that I Saw Once Off Mexico 69
Astrological Reflections on the Occasion of my 30th Birthday . .71

V "As Senator from Carthage . . ."

The Senator from Carthage 75
The Near Sierra 76
John Chrysostom 83
The Stamp Catalogue 84
Poem Addressed to my Father and his Friends 85
I Weep for Whales 87
Concerning my Sudden Retirement from Public Life 88

VI "I descended the ladder, down . . ."

The Oracle of Trophonius 91
Childhood II 92
Song for the Angel 93
Concerning Destinations 95
The Catch is 97
California Burial 98
Mail, for Jaime 100
The Expulsion 102

VII "searching for her . . ."

Magdalene 105
Autumnal 107
The Complaints that Women Have Are Real 108
In the Provinces 109
Actaeon 110
After Venus, I loved the Mediterranean 112

VIII "I'd like to draw some conclusion from this . . ."

For Jaime, at home 115
Taos Spring 116
Ditch Cleaning 117
The Unborn Father to the Mother of his Child 119
A Moment in Three Lives 121
Dust Devils, and Other Forms 122
For my Daughter, an Apology 124
Emergence 125

Epilogue

The Fool 131

Appendix

Easter Sunday, Cordoba 135

Envoi 137

Soulscot

Ceremony

The burial of the dead
tongues again.

I descend
into the clutter of monuments,
and gather
into my body
the old life I find there:
these poems
that are anatomy,
complaint,
and autobiography;

and together we shall die
and be put to rest;
and when that's done,
I shall be born again,
and shall rise speaking
the first word,
the sound made new again.

I

"the Warrior Boy named Darkness . . ."

Poise, a Cowboy Poem

I sit, back to wall,
face to door,
not short not tall,
not much at all,
just me alone,
not more,
not less,
feet on the floor,
eyes on the door,
my soul quite still,
awaiting death,
who shoots to kill.

A Nativity: L. A. 1940

I see a quaint tableau
in the back of the old dog's
dying brain: it's the Holy Family
gathered around a pile of dung
and other things
under an ulcerous nite sky in L. A.
The sky is lit
by neon, kleig lights,
and the Goodyear blimp,
which is announcing
—whose arrival?—
why mine, of course.
Sanctus, Sanctus
the angels sang;
he's here at last,
and he's a little nuts.

But love me, love my dog,
the dangerous one;
he's got the whole nativity
in his mind and can't forget
the way it was:
the cars, the camels,
and the three wise men
(my gym teacher, banker,
and psychiatrist,
who presented me at birth
with a magical pen
which writes large still
in salt water
these words: *Do, Don't,*
Death, and *Us).*
A holy night; and all the while

the Bow Wow with the bad heart
was howling carols into the air
assuring mother, father,
the neighbors, and the cops
that he, the dog, was still there—
chained up behind the house
with the Holy Family lodged in his mind
like a sharp bone
in the throat.
   Poor dog; I had to kill him:
he bit the postman on the tit
when he was delivering the Xmas mail—
the calendar from the Company
and more of Hallmark's bullshit
about the precious Baby
and his Mom and Dad.

Childhood I

I say quickly to my bear,
shhh:
      and I clap my hand
across his mouth
for we hear the thunder moving
in the darkened house.
And we hear our hearts beating.
Then voices.
      We stop.
And then we hear the distant
rolling growl
of war.
      And the sound the lightning
makes, the stroke
descending.
      Listen,
now it hammers on the altar stone,
now it tears the clouds apart.
I am afraid
of how the towns are burning,
and how the towers fall.
Through the smoke
the voices drone and weep
and call.
      I remember how,
if I should die,
or my heart should break,
I pray the lord
my soul to take.

      I am afraid
of blood when I'm alone,
and shut my eyes.
But bear and I together
are not afraid,

and we will see it all someday,
how the bodies are
and how they die.
I think they make a hole
and the words run out,
but I am not sure.
They are hidden now
in sheets so I cannot see.
They're shrouded, the grownups say.

Hurry, Bear;
we slip past the door.

My father is away
on a rolling ship,
and the house is mine.
For years I've sailed the house
on this child-dark sea.
It is full of monsters
and I call it
Terrible Lake Silence.
Upstairs and downstairs
and across it
I've wandered.
           Listen
I know a nursery rhyme
about how I'm born,
but I forget the words.
Behind the door, inside,
began the Warrior Boy
named Darkness, me.

I am invisible;
I will write a poem someday.

But I am an egg and break apart.
The king's horses
and the king's men
are waiting in the hall.

They follow me.
The hall is endless,
the darkness weeps for something,
I don't know what.
Bear says,
The darkness weeps for you.
Because I'm born? I ask.
Yes, says bear.

(All this happens
late in forty-four.
    I wandered often
in the darkness of that year:
boy and stuffed bear
shivering in the dark halls
of a large house
somewhere in America.
It was on the coast,
I think. Those were fearful
times;
                and I wept
for all the incomprehensible
tragedies, for the Jews
and for Poland; and
for horses, cows, and children
lying shot and frozen in the snow,
while behind them,
in the photograph,
the house and stables burned;
and for the sounds I heard, somehow,
of armor clanking,
and of planes whining, coming in
low over the pine tops.
It was a merciless education.
    And the first Christmas
I remember was also forty-four.
I remember that I received

a helmet and a wooden reduction
of the Springfield rifle.
That rifle is as vivid to me today
as if I were, at this very moment,
cradling it in my hands.
Christmas: the ribbons
on the little tree,
the carved German figures
in rigid parody of Christ's birth,
the toy rifle, the flesh
of red apples—
all mimed peacefully
against the backdrop
of the destruction of Europe
which, as far as I knew,
was in the next county.
Because of all this
I know that there is something
that I shall never forget.
It comes from being born into
what Papa calls, "the most difficult time
we've had since the dark ages."
It is still difficult.
    There are survivors of my childhood,
real and imaginary ones.
Bear now
is the companion of my daughter,
who, like I was then, is four).

Shhhh, I say to Bear;
we hear the noise again.
And we descend.
       In a closet
beneath the stair,

the darkmost hole
in all the house,
I hide my bear.
He is running for his life;
the King would take him
to the Hall of Mammals
and kill him there.
But you are safe now, Bear,
and fast asleep.
And I go back upstairs alone.
I go past the door,
it's quiet now.
At last the night has come
to claim the house.
I swear into the night's ear
that I will never tell
the things I've seen,
that I will love my bear,
that I will not run away
nor break apart.

      And now
I'll close my eyes,
but I'll wake up soon
for morning starts. See,
I told you so,
I did not die.
I have this tiny cross.
It protects me;
see, it opens:
inside
is my father's voice
and a dry relic
of my mother's heart.

1943

I killed snails for a penny a dozen.
I put salt in their foot-wound
and watched them die
bubbling;
                    and I remember
fierce doves in the old pine
at the end of the yard,
and the smell of cut grass,

and lace curtains,
laundered thin. They move;
grandmother calls from the window,
come home,

                    to the house,
to the roses in room shadow,
the talcum smells, and portraits
of forgotten men.

And now mother calls,
an air-raid tonight, the warnings,
my love, come home,
to the house;

                    and I did;
and they drew black curtains
across the window, and they told me
that there were planes overhead;

and I crawled among women
in warm beds; and each night
I dreamt of a wild stag, how it raged
through the garden

                    pulling stars
and birds from the highest trees.
Its towering antlers
were stained with blood.

1944

I remember the fourth summer
of the war.
I remember the drone
of insects,
and the garden dying
in the heat.
And in that garden I remember
a weedy pond
whose oily water
was stirred only
by the slow strokes
of Japanese goldfish.
And I remember dragonflies
hurrying along the surface
of the pond,
and hovering over lilypads,
their wings veined
and helicopterish.

I do not remember my father
in the war,
and I didn't know exactly
which war he was in.
But I do remember my grandfather;
how small my hand seemed
in his; how often
he cried out
in his sleep;
and how he seemed
to fear something
in the black pond's
depth.

II

"Death is obsessed with me . . ."

Crow's Version

In this white rush
of funeral morning,
this royal sunlight,
the crow gleams.
His feathers
are engraved pitch
and his beak
is purest ivory,

but black,
like the God's heart.
Crow is our best bird,
the pit herald
who speaks
the last word.
And now
he bestows laughter

upon Pharoah,
upon his coach
and crown,
and upon the ministers,
Lord Finance,
Public Words,
and Exterior,
who are all dead

and buried together
like Egyptians,
which they are;
and his bright
black eye,
the darkest jade
beneath
blue heaven

saw the sky crack
over fly-stung hill
called Golgotha,
saw the Christ
falter,
the forsaking,
saw God's man-eye
dim

forever;
and he heard lamentations,
the victims weeping
after Rolling Thunder,
and he heard
the iron breathing
in the throat
of empire;

and he heard
the merchant's wheedle,
and the king's belch,
and the prince whining
that he had not enough;
and he heard the creak
of armies moving,
and of armies settling

into seige.
And he flew
through the smoke
of cities burning,
and he fed easily
on the man flesh,
for death
is everywhere

at pride's end,
and a man is meat
like a sheep's head;
and perching
in the cool pine,
heart pure as ever,
he saw
the plague roost

in the man house,
and in the lung
and lymph;
and descending
from the tree
he plucked the bishop's
velvet eye
from the mud;

and he rose, startled
by the new noise
of locomotives,
looms, mills,
the engines
moaning
above the Mount of Olives;
and he heard again

the gnashing
of the man beast,
as he proclaims that greed
is good and right,
as he feeds crow cake
and garbage
along trade's edge;
and crow scavenged

in trenches,
amidst armored litter
and patented devices,
some that have not yet
exploded;
and death
was everywhere again,
and crow was everywhere,

perching on the spires
of Chartres
and on the chimneys
of Treblinka;
and the recounting
ends;
and I call out
in my nightmare,

Crow, be witness
to modern times,
to the black clouds
of the burning
dead,
the millions
dead
in my generation.

For Jaime, in Mexico

Death is obsessed with me,
and I think with you.
There is no trail I take
through the cactus
that does not lead to a carcass
or to a cleaned skin.
And there are no words between us
that don't come eventually
to a natural end.

Cerberus to the Mole

Three dog death
who guards the hole
asks a favor
of the dirt dark mole:

A kindness, burrower,
I ask of you:
lend your blindness
to those with eyes,
that once they're dead
and shoveled down,
they will not know
they're underground.

In the Tropics

The devil, damn him,
knows my hunger
for a glimpse of him.
And so he set upon me
with a scene
that I'll not forget
in a lifetime of watching
for his tracks:

for it was he, surely,
in the goat's form,
who ran bleating
through the yard
and upset the plate of guavas
from the bench:
the tin plate clattered
and eight guavas
went rolling in the dust.
And from the house
came an old woman,
a slave's daughter,
the lover and keeper
of the fruit.
And from the house also
came a small boy,
his belly swollen
with the worm or hunger.
And the boy, with a stick,
fell upon the first guava,
striking it until the juice flowed
and, gaining strength,
he thrashed into the second,
mangling its flesh, while
the old woman, shuffling

her bare feet against the ground,
cried out to the Holy Mother,
that She protect the fruit.
But the boy, now frenzied, flailed
into the third, spattering
the green pulp and seeds
on his solemn face.
The old woman, weeping,
fell to the dirt, clutching
just two guavas
to her dry breast.
And the boy thrashed with his stick
until he had destroyed
the three guavas that remained.
The old woman's tears
flowed into the red dust of the island.
The boy, panting, licked
the juice from his arm.
The goat bleated,
and in his voice was laughter.

Death in Mexico

From Juarez,
at the cancer clinic,
his wife writes north to us:
"how well," she says,
"I've come to know
this shabby town,
its dilapidation,
its smells of dust and dung.
On cold mornings
the city lies beneath a pall
of charcoal smoke;
it curls from the earth
like incense
from a censer.
I dreamt last night
of a train of mules
that pulled a hearse,
and though I saw it clearly,
all I knew of it
was smell—smell
of mule breath,
of matted hair,
and earth.

"Jasper is almost gone now.
You **would** not know him,
so old and gaunt
he has become.
Though drugged,
he talks clearly
of going home;
he wants to die
in the mountains.
But we are here;

we listen
through the window
to the clang of trolleys
and the snarl of trucks.
All day I read to him
from the El Paso Times.
It doesn't help
or matter, so we wait.
Some people from Oregon
told us about this place,
about how they cure death here
with seeds. We came,
but it was too late.

"I will leave him here,
in Mexico,
when at last he dies.
I can't bring him home
because the money's gone.
I had to bribe the guards
when I brought him south,
because we had no visa.
And when we crossed the river
the beggars below the bridge
called out to us.
They were naked boys
with long nets:
soul catchers, Jasper said,
throw them something,
they look hungry.
So I threw them
all the coins I had,
money I knew I'd need
to bring him home to burial
in the forgotten mountains,
home to the land
of clean snow."

Jeremiad

Manhattan pukes
its unholy muck
into the Atlantic,
its gutted livestock,
ladies' hearts,
poisons, money,
clogged arteries,
dead birds,
and filth;

and a red blossom,
like tuberculosis,
unfolds on the cheek
of the world;

and the fat fish
of the judgment
lays its sacred mouth
on the dragging flesh
of this raving harlot;

and the crabs bubbling
at land's edge
sing the Office
of the Dead;

They sing,
you shall be pulled down,
all of you,
into the sea.

Intimations

The lantern,
lurching against the night
and thickets,
picked up the glint of eyes.
A fox, perhaps,
or a cat.

The air was clear.
Beyond the far edge of the sea,
the silent flicker of a squall.
Turning inland,
and through the scrub
that lined the beach,
I felt the spacious terror
of the darkness,
and of the blind stars glinting,
watching me.

And in the old house
I smelled rotting flesh.
A squirrel, perhaps,
dead in the wall.

Elegy

Death

She was young, and I remember
how she was: tall and beautiful
and full of gentle irony and sudden laughter.
But her veins were breaking,
and at the end she became a memory
of herself, a retreating voice
that asked the reason for her life.
She clung to us for days
until at last she received an answer:
the strokes of the village bell
announcing that she was dead.

Burial

We carried her up the dry hill
above the summer fields
and buried her with the others.
and after we had spoken words
we threw earth into the dark hole,
and the clods falling fell
upon the pine box we had made;
and the sound returning
was hollow and wood dull,
as if darkness itself had rung,
resonant of all that was and is not.

Transfiguration

In this unkept camposanto,
beneath the bitter range,
we leave our sister.

The one fresh mound is hers;
it lies east to west.
Death is endless departure;
it is not rest. It is the end.
And we painted on a scrap of wood
the words we said, but to these
there is no answer. The words are plain,
Farewell, Sandra, friend.

Death, Listen

Death, listen,
I've had this to say
for twenty years,
but each time I tried before
I lost my nerve.
This time I won't,
so listen, Death,
I do not like you,
not even a little;
and I want with all my heart
to make you sting.

So now I'll begin my cast.
You are a mean man, Death;
you charge high interest
for this brief loan
called life.
And you use our bodies,
so we call you pimp.
What do you say to that,
Comrade Death?

    Nothing, yet?
I am too polite perhaps;
I'll try again.
You are a fawning salesman,
peddling quicklime
and insurance
to soldiers in a trench.
And you are the Black Pope;
you crop flesh
instead of souls,
and that is small
and cheap. And, Christ,
how stinks your breath.
What now, Old Death?

Nothing yet?
Indeed, you offend slowly.
They warned me.
But I am not down;

I shall raise my voice.
You are an obese crow,
your beak glistens
with the grease of carrion.

You deaf, arrogant bastard,

you are a blind cat, without
a tongue, stealing
eggs from the wren's nest.
you are a muddy hole
filled with rain.

But no, I can not provoke you,
can I? Then listen,
Death,

I concede.
I admit that you are limitless.
I know because I've never met a man
who wasn't yours.
There, is that enough?
Do I yield enough?

No, not.
You want my life,
and tribute too?

My Lord, then,
I concede again:
you are the king's pay
and the poor man's heaven,

you are the right hand
and the left hand,

you are the fulfillment
and the wheel,

and the word made flesh.

Enough, enough.
I beg now, answer me
the one question
that I've always had.
Let me hear it
in your own voice.

Death,
what conceivable need
do you have of us?

III

"I sense the continent diminish . . ."

In Boston Common

I walk among the graves
in Boston Common.
The names I read are English,
except for one Chinese:
Chow Mandarien,
who sailed in 1789
on the strange seas of his time
from Canton to Boston.
This frail yellow man
was called one night and fell
from the high crosstree
to the polished deck below.
It was by his master's kindness,
the stone says,
that he was thus moored to earth
in Massachussets.

On Mount Tamalpais

We rest on an ancient slope,
on serpentine,
among scrub manzanita,
surrounded by sweet water,
springs among trees.
Below us, a gull rests
on the rising wind.
Regard,
the waves of the sea
against the land.
I sense the continent diminish—
the Sacramento carrying
the mountains to the sea,
and the limestone cliffs
flaking into the surf
of California.
I think
of all the creatures
that have died.
I think of a pile of oyster shells
coming apart
in the sun.

August in Oklahoma

I have seen no trees
on sixty long horizons,
no grove of shade on soil
that's red and burns
with the name of August.
I have had no rest, have seen
no beast that lives. It is
the season of the dead tortoise,
when time is told by water
falling in the mind.
In the distant south the flat sky
takes clouds on its dry shell;
but the glide of thunder
over many miles
relieves not heat
nor failing heart.

Sky Full of Beasts

Sky full of beasts,
singing.
Trees full of insects,
singing. A slow
moon rising.
September.
The earth falls, how
shall I say it,
into patient sadness.
Insects everywhere,
in trees,
beneath rocks,
in the cooling water,
dying.

The Encantadas

September turns the land mass sullen;
the sea sours,
and slows our passage
to the isles.
In this dim venture,
distance lays out his child
upon the sea,
and we cannot believe,
and our voyage fails.

In La Mancha

Sitting, as the night fell,
in a crumbling place
above the dying jungle
of the day, we talked
of lions. *O to see a lion,*
you, the dreamer, said.

But there were no lions
in those home close fields;
there were rabbits only,
and startled doves,
and the twilight rustling
in the olive groves.

And at the far edge
of the day's light
and of the possible,
we saw a solitary hunter.
He was returning home.
He'd seen no lions either.

Poem about the Water

My neighbor came today
to complain, as he does each year,
about the government,
which is ignorant and remote,
about the porcupine
that eats his corn,

and about the water,
which is not enough.
  *They take more than is theirs
upstream,* he says.
  Come then, we'll go, I say,
*and talk to them again,
especially to Romero,
who has no paper for his water.
  And someday,* my neighbor says,
*we will take the rifle,
and not the paper.*

And so we went,
in his old truck, which remembers,
he always says,
when the water was high in the ditches,
and remembers Roosevelt,
and hauled bricks for the W.P.A.
The grass, he says,
from here to Antonito,
stood to the running boards
in the old days.

We went
as we have gone before,
tired and resolute, and grim
as farmers. The dust of the road

coated our faces,
as with pollen
for the ceremonies of middle summer.
And his brown dog
prowled behind us on the wooden truck bed,
alert with anticipation.

* *

The sheriff came today,
with questions.
I showed him the ditch,
which is not wet,
and the corn leaves
which are dry as treaties.
They, upstream, say this,
and you say different,
he says.

And I say,
we went about the water,
as we do each year
in middle summer.
We took the paper.
We did nothing.

Can I see the dog?
he says. *No,* I say,
and point to where we'd buried
him in the sage.

When we did
I could not look,
for the familiar head
had been shattered
by a rifle bullet.
We wrapped the stiff body
in a grain sack and laid it
gently, three feet down.

We were in Romero's yard,
standing in the sun by the truck.
Romero said
that he did not take too much,
and that his corn was nearly dead.
Then the shot came,
from the ditch bank,
a good shot, a hundred yards.
It was not Romero
because we were with him.

We will have a meeting tonight
in the school house, my neighbor says.
We will decide what to do.
We will read the paper again,
as we have many times before.
The paper says the water belongs
to our valley; and it always did
until so many farms came in
above us. We will decide, as always,
to do nothing.
The government does nothing.
They pave roads we will never use.

Drought

A dry time
for a long time.
Ninety days without rain.
The dust rising
and filling a thousand miles
of sky.
The cowboy says,
"We can hold on,
rock bottom,
ten days more,
then we sell."

The papers say
it's the worst time
in sixty years,
since the records began:
cracked earth
and cows dying;
ranches folding
and the people
moving to the jobs
in Lubbock
and El Paso.

Then rain.
A great cloud
rolling out of the Guadalupes
and across the Pecos.
Rain clattering on the roof.
We push up the window
and watch the stain spread
on the ground.
I ask if he thinks God
is in the thunder.
He says *yes.*

IV

"the strike of intellect upon the stone . . ."

Know This

Know this:

that the strike of intellect
upon the stone
throws no light
into the great darkness;

and know also in your heart,
that believing
will not lift off
the weight of God's neglect.

The Holy Man

Old Juan Ocampo
is drunk again.
He sits in the middle
of his bleak yard
while dust, chickens,
dogs, and children
revolve around him.
He removes,
one by one,
the spokes
of a bicycle
wheel.
He says he does it
to confuse the Lord.

The Dice and Sunday

I risk judgement and let Sunday pass
by staying home and rolling dice.
My room is locked, door
to jamb; the window's tight
against the holy air that's so
bright and cold outside,
that's as high and blue

as heaven. I drink an ordinary
wine and drop the bones against
the table. I seek perfection, eleven,
but get stomach gas, a little
premonition of old age. But
thinking still of heaven, I attend
to church out of season and

commune vaguely by reading graves.
The suicides are outside the wall
and those within are christian
and respectable—the captain
of industry, beloved wife,
the child taken into the bosom
of heaven—all seem dead equally

to me, but I am not sure. But
gambling still, I stay inside
on Sunday, and through the window
watch the faithful wander home
from the weekly prayers
that speak our wistful search
for life beyond the belly, beyond

old age and death. But I'll not
risk church; I'd catch my last disease
in the tired hope of Sunday's air.
And since it's quiet and warm
within my skin, I ignore the meaning
in the bones—the random
omen in throws of dice,

a throw of nothing, twice.

Spinoza's Dog

Spinoza sez
it's angels descending
that make the air move,
and from angels,
breezily
he deduces for us
God.
But it was his dog
who actually saw Him,
saw the Boots,
and Trouser Legs,
and the Flexed Knees,
from the superior vantage
of being beneath
the writing desk.

China Always is Near

I read once,
in a treatise on Tu Fu,
that in the Chinese language
there is only one tense,
the restless
and eternal present.
I sat a long time
at my desk
and thought about it.

And while I did,
an architecture
of wind and black cloud
and rain
was built in the east
behind the house.
I heard it
roaring, lamenting,
and rejoicing.

Years have passed,
and that ancient storm
is with me still.
It has become
an indestructable occurrence
in my life,
an enduring articulation,
like the Great Wall,
or the sound of Tu Fu's voice.

To a Great Sea Tortoise
that I Saw Once
off Mexico

The sea lay polished flat
within me,
and formed until today
the most perfect horizon
in the world.
And I believed the sea
because I'd sailed in boats
upon it. But now I'm told
by you, O Tortoise,
that the sea curves
inside me

like the liquid rolling surface
of my eye.
And I believe you,
because you have crossed
the sea alive
and lived within it.
And so today
the level world
is conceived again
and becomes a living sphere
inside me.

Tortoise, you have changed me;
I have felt the swimming of your soul
inside me. But now you go away;
you breach the circle
of my love and mind, and begin
departure along your ancient way.
I weep to let you go;
and a vast salt world

is released at last
from where it's grown
inside me.

From the beach I watched an hour
as you labored through the surf
and out to sea,
as you swam away
toward that more perfect coast
that you alone can find.
Its wonder lies, I know,
beyond my compass
of the world.
It lies far to seaward
and beyond me.

Astrological Reflections
on the Occasion of my 30th Birthday

I am born in the sign
of the double fish,
the deformed foot,
and the nailed hand.
I am born in the Horsemen,
with Lucifer crossed
in the Dog Star
at the lean edge.

And in conjunction
Sagittarius is released,
its trajectory closing.
And at rear stage center,
Corvus the Emperor
is tuning his fiddle.

These signs,
which mean nothing,
revolve
around some inconceivable
pivot,
to what may be
the divine music.

I have listened for the tune.
I have heard no tune.
But I have heard the Maestro snarling
from time to time.

V

"As Senator from Carthage . . ."

The Senator from Carthage

As Senator from Carthage
I proposed a blood tax
on salt, a tax on those
who mine it,
on those who sell it.
Tears exempted.
                    I recall
sitting on a fallen column and
watching the Mediterranean fleet
steaming toward Gibralter,
plowing the sea with iron.
And I recalled what was done, the war,
and the people voting in the darkness,
salt jamming the machines.

The Near Sierra

For Chile,
For Neruda.

I

I begin in Spanish, *por respeto,*
and tell how Lorca died,
como fue asesinado en Granada por fascistas,
como las mariposas cayeron hacia la tierra,
con sus cantos tapados in their yellow throats,
and how his last rites were spoken
en las lenguas ignorantes de este siglo,
the language of the nocturnal pistol . . .
   Federico, poet,
dead of politics in his prime,
his life cut off at the singing throat,
dead of the black *guardia*
      civil   O tales
we will never know
    of the Alhambra,
    of that night in July,
    nineteen
    thirty six,
when Spain began to fall,
when Federico's last poems
    were lost.

Cold dirt for his mouth.
No flowers for his mouth.
Our words not near sufficient.
And his grave, too,
    is lost,
    somewhere
below the Andaluz sierra.

And we too are insufficient,
and so must invent him
     dying,
     again and again,
     and now again,
him saying,
"Remember me, *Hermano,*
and the fine days we knew together
     in Madrid,
     in the old days,
before the world was burning."

II

Spain's been dead a long time now,
and Lorca's gone to some fierce musical
heaven,   with gypsies and green bells;
and besides,
I was not yet born in '36;
and since then
I've gotten cynical . . .

I was in Mexico, the Capitol,
when Chile fell.
And in the Plaza de Madrid
I heard an old music rising
in an open throat.
I heard workers
drumming with bones
on the furnaces
and smokestacks of the city,
and on the aqueducts,
and on the leaves falling
in Chapultepec Park.
and I heard the singing
in the blood:

"This bone is my Indian father.
This bone my shin.
The butterfly with the feathered
soul   becomes the eagle
and shall rise again."

. . . and I saw the papers. Dateline,
Santiago, Reuters:
"Army suspends liberties in Chile.
Allende dies
as planes strafe palace."
                                    Well,
I thought,
it's Guernica again,
the stukas savaging democracy,
    the planes driven
by vast
international   engines.
        /and dateline,
New York:
"Internationals are up again,
and copper up.
The Escudo firms.
Credits will be restored,
a spokesman said . . ."
                            . . . so
the United Fruit Company
is harvesting the heartland again.
And whatever else
did you expect of us?

And my wife, who's Mexican,
wept when Chile fell,
    said, "Each indian woman
is the widow of Allende;"
and cried, as if I had done it,

"Pero Zapata vive
with the angels,
in all the vast heart
of the sierra."

          With his barefoot angels,
          in the near   sierra.

III

Latin America
is no abstraction,
no political conception,
not just market and material,
not simply geographical profusion.
It is people;
and they live, many,
      very   hard,
and sleep
      beneath lean   stars.
Chile's failure
is our failure.
It will come back to haunt us;
it will hammer at the gates.
Latin America, my brother Yanquis,
is the near   sierra.

IV

His excellency the Ambassador,
Citizen Neruda is dead.
Don Pablo is dead.
That singular voice.
He is dead, they say, of cancer;
or of death, perhaps,
compounded by a broken heart.
Or of moral obligation.

And when he died
the hollow filled with a rushing
sound   of swords and greed.
And of the many voices
that were waiting beyond the door,
that were singing to the darkness.
These are the choirs of Babel
            and of the future.

                    V

. . . and tell again
what happened when Neruda died:
how the black *guardia* came,
            as in his dream,
and broke through the doors
of his empty house;
how they, the deaf men
of steel and mule skin,
the librarians of death
and gasoline . . .
                    Listen,
to the hooves clattering
in the courtyard,
the click of rifle bolts, and thump
of spear butt against the gate.
Voices fester in the darkness,
            vicious laughter
            in the darkness
            beyond the circle of light;
and the fire illuminates
            the uniforms again,
            and the men,
            with their black
            unpronounceable tongues,
            utter the darkness
            from their wax-white heads.

"*Sargento, sargento,*
      and these wooden angels,
      them too?"
And the sergeant,
presiding in the robes of the red
bishop, says,
"Burn everything you can.
Burn what will."
And they burned
his desk and the cane chair,
and a carving in ironwood
of San Raphael holding
the two fishes.
And when the fire burned well,
they threw in his books:
        (The dawn
breaks   over the Andes,)
and the smoke is dark with
the rare Bordeaux edition
of Montaigne, 1588;
and with a soldier's copy of *"Espana
en el Corazon"* that had survived,
   in the man's pocket,
the Zaragoza front
and the Pyrenees;   and
in manuscript
poems,   unfinished,
of the wind bending
toward the Southern Cross; and
last letters in Lorca's hand.
This is the sacrament
of ignorance   and obedience,
   its smoke rising
over the roof tops. And the wind
descending from the ridge
of the continent,   smelling
first of snow,

then rain,   scatters
the hieroglyphic ash
out to sea.   O tales
we will never know
   of Chile,
   of those September nights
   in Seventy-Three.

VI

The black detachments
are at the gates again.
They have risen, like the buzzard phoenix,
from the ash of the best men.
And though their faiths differ,
as do currencies   and skin,
their heart of ceremony is ancient,
and reoccuring:

they are burning the world.
And they are burning
Buenos Aires, and Prague,
Manilla, Moscow, Boston,
Jerusalem, Seoul, Belfast
Santiago, and Madrid.

And they are burning
the rain
         and the sea
and the wind.

John Chrysostom

John, how the people moved you!
They filled your mouth
with their dumb ears,
and you sent them into the city
with your heart beating
in their sack shirts,
and they slaughtered jews.

Later, at supper, I was surprised
to hear your golden tongue
clack, like an oar out of lock,
against the wooden spoon.

The Stamp Catalogue

Wilson in the hall of mirrors,
the vermillion error, voided
and withdrawn;
Eisenhower on Utah Beach,
cancelled;
and Irish rose, red stains;
a dry Spanish commemorative,
cancelled brutally;
Queen Elizabeth II, the silver
wedding, sixpence, a sentimental
favorite;
a classic French colonial,
devalued on the face;
the Apollo XII Devotional,
New Guinea, a fine example;
the giant Mongul horseman,
mint, rising in the east.

Poem Addressed to my Father and his Friends

Father,
it's a bad age we're in,
but you deny it. You remain
the optimist, a kind of virgin,
religiously ignorant.
But listen, can't you hear
the wind rising in the ass end
of your golden calf? It's a foul wind
and brings death to many
by poison, famine,
or profitable calculation.

But you hear nothing.
You have retired to the shelter
of the first class compartment,
and there you entertain the ladies
with your mechanical fictions
of the better mousetrap,
or mineshaft, or memory bank;

and you retell, again and again,
the old romance
of the ultimate moonstone,
how it contains elixirs
whose uses are surely marvelous
though not yet known.

And the ladies applaud carefully
and dispense the sacraments
from the picnic basket:
a pale Chateau Corruption, 1950;
the Christ cake drained chemically
of all nutrition;
and dolphin tongues on toast.

Father, though I love
some part of you,
when I hear you talking
I am reminded of the scene
in the unpublished works
of Voltaire
where Dr. Pangloss masturbates
to pass the time
while his train
is stalled in hell.

I Weep for Whales

I weep
for the death of trees,

and for the sea broken
into zones of trade,
into routes for oil,
and into east/west
of Greenwich time;

and I weep for the sky
gone wrong,
filled with burning wings;

but most of all
I weep for whales,
who are killed with cannons
for their precious song.

Concerning my Sudden Retirement from Public Life.

Each morning
I rolled off the bed,
fluffed my feathers and,
like a mad goose,
set out to peck to death
a glacier.
Each day's agony
was a trifle;
the aggregate, however,
of those five years . . . .

Brothers,
forgive me;
I was tired
and nearly crazy.

VI

"I descended the ladder, down . . ."

The Oracle of Trophonius

(After Pausanius IX, 39)

For S. Frazier

I descended the ladder, down
through the stone hole, then
headfirst,
      through the snake's
passage, into the earthen darkness
of the coiled palace.
And there, underground,
in the presence of a voice
resembling water, the voice
of the Oracle of Trophonius,
I stayed a day and a night;

And in the pitch blackness,
I listened without distraction
to the voice. I felt
the sacred presence
of the serpents, how
they pulled down upon my feet
like the hands of a terrible mother.
I fed them honey-cakes
and they released me; and
because my heart was pure,
they returned me to the world
neither dead nor mad.

When I emerged into stoney Boeotia,
the women carried me
to a lighted room
and there they nurse me.
Soon I will be healed;
and when I am
I shall reveal the words
I spoke and heard
in the presence of Trophonius.
Only then will I remember
how to laugh and sing again.

Childhood II

The cat plays drums.
The rat rolls up the rug
and prays. The cockroach
sidles toward its hole.
The dogs, all dead,
stand around in shades of air
and cry.
      And mother
sleeps inside the box,
beneath the board, in light
that seeps from jars, RX,
hair of the same dog, O
beasts, old friends, dear
dead dogs. Sounds in the big
house, darkness; I, small,
hand on bannister, descend.

Song for the Angel

Listen, and I will tell
how the grey wings, the visitation
drew near; how the wind breath
blew with some quality
of death I knew before,
but now have lost. Wind

groaning
in the eucalyptus, sap smell,
moon gleaming on the rocks
at lakeside,
         the wound dark,
blood dried. I did not move.

I am at lake's edge now;
I am reading Yeats, then
poem sound: The wind
and lap of water
on smooth stone.
I listen, heart full
of moving air,
first to life,
to language next,
and wind. I search
for the quality
of confluent time. The warm
wind slides
across the lake, leaves
faint grey tracks
of air.

A thousand
thousand
doves
startle from the dark blood
ground. Before each flew
I saw its eye.
               And now
an angel steps toward shore,
two shining fish in hand,

and he is cut down quick
with knives,
among the trees,
in that lake's edge
bloody wood.

The mocking bird
doth sing.
I do not move.

Concerning Destinations

Our instincts are corrupt,
but they guide us still
to surprising destinations.

Thus, the sailor
rarely finds himself,
but finds, instead,
by accident, the source
of spice, passage
between islands, the Antilles
and Manilla, and becomes
at last, the Navigator,
in green bronze.

Thus also, Dante
Alighieri, inclined at first
toward her, the lady,
toward her flesh principally;
     but as that port eluded,
the sailor became a poet;   and,
as consumation kept off longer,
failure became the divine fragrance
that induced madness
and the gradual release of self
toward exotic imaginations
of heaven and hell, and finally,
toward his highest self
in art.

And thus, inescapably, Saul,
who, while voyaging
toward Port Damascus, saw

extraordinary light, saw himself
the sinner bound for hell,
saw the bruised god
resurrected and in heaven,
who then became himself,
Saint Paul.

Thus destiny, perhaps:
We become who we are.

The Catch is . . .

The catch is
that I can not be
who I am not.
And now,
if I can find who I am not,
I shall at least
be spared the embarrassment
of becoming the wrong person.

California Burial

We move the body.
It comes behind us in the box,
wrapped in Turkish towels.
    South now,
past the steambaths,
and the stucco palaces
of pink and umber,
then west,
across Pico and Sepulveda,

heat beating on the black
cars
        and singing
in the velveteen ears
of the hearse.   These
faint sweet smells
of disinfectant
and asphalt,   and hum
of tires along the arteries
of L.A.,
            surf
of diseased blood
in my ears.
                And south again,
along the monotonous avenues

lined with palm
and parrot feathers,
and into the plaster of paris hills
of Hollywood.

To graveside,
the soundstage for her departure,
where the Sun King
and Valentino
moonlight as sadness
in this gray metallic glare.
And now
onto the real grass,
as we follow the coffin
toward its precise hole,
    in this winter burial
    of my grandmother
    in California.

Mail, for Jaime

The letter that I sent you in Morocco
that was lost
contained news of such pain
that it's better lost.
Better, to spare you;
but still,
Rabat seems the wrong place
for those words to die,
to fall out of orbit,
or into the hands of God . . .

what does happen,
I wonder,
to those words that no one hears,
and how
does each silence occur?

Not that it much matters.
There is more important news than mine;
you must listen for it.
The dry wind, for instance,
off the Sahara,
contains more of substance
than I do.
        But still,
I seldom write,
and when I do, it matters:
my news is what I am,
or is, at least, what I think I am,
or what I can bring myself to say.
In the missing letter
I said that I am alone,

that I am conscious of the pain I cause;
I said that my child, your god-child,
has fallen on the thorny ground
of the life I lead.
And I said that the crops
have failed this year:
you would not recognize
our sometimes green
now bitter valley.

Do you see what I mean?
Such news is better lost.
Do you agree?
Answer please.
And I'd like to know
if the malaria has left you yet,
and does the blood pound still
in your head. And what
have you found to read
on the Silent Continent?

And lastly,
tell me of the Red Sea,
which lies north and east
of where I believe you are.
Make me believe it's real,
and that one of us, at least,
is listening.

The Expulsion

The sword cools
and the pain subsides;
and with the bloody gate
so far behind,
I lay me down for sleeping
on the hot flint:

    and I dwell upon the grief
    that unfolds within,
    that though I am born again
    and seem immortal
    in the word's precision,
    I cannot forget
    our loss of Eden.
    Nor can I forget
    that self knows self so simply:
    as an eloquent and thoughtful insect
    stuck on death's pin.

VII

"searching for her . . ."

Magdalene

I am young
and I am flesh;
and choirs of whores
attend to me
in Times Square.
And she, among the women,
was beautiful:
not twenty, lean
as a running beast,
and blond as sunlight.

But New York is real,
and I saw the tracks
of a dark longing
upon her arm, and melancholy
had webbed her in.
   We retired
from the glitterish city
of the plain
and took sanctuary
in a pale blue room

above the din
of forty-second street.
She disrobed;
and by a light
that hung from heaven
at the end of a long cord
I saw her perfect soul revealed,
and her flesh
transformed.
You are beautiful

as the Eucharist,
I said; and
as I guttered
my faint light into her,
she, my sallow angel,
performed the miracle of love
within me;
and I thought,
forgive me, woman,
for I will deny you soon.

Autumnal

October's come,
and as the sun slides south
toward some distant summer,
it leaves behind for us
a light so clear
that it gives,
beyond my poor power
of self-delusion,
great worth to us,
to our frail and hopeless
grapplings,
these acts called love.
And in time I see
that this autumn light
shall form a golden drop
around us two,
and we shall be as Sheba's
fornicating flies
caught in an amber bead.

The Complaints that Women Have Are Real

Love,
first thrashed out
in a car, could never,
sadly, be the same for her;
her downy hopes
of what might have been
beat and flopped,
then ceased to stir.
And he, spent,
but unsatisfied,
discarded her,
feeling somehow
that she had cheated him.
He wiped off,
buttoned up,
but romantic still,
moved on
to assault again.

In the Provinces

Damp wind
among the cabbage rows.
Dead fish, belly up,
on the high sand,
above the tide.
Gulls
with yellow beaks
pluck out the eyes,
and reach neatly
to the innards.

I bicycle
to the woman's house,
a mile from the sea.
(I have forgotten her name.)
She plucks at my heart;
I open her belly.
We are feeding.

Actaeon

The last of daylight
lingers in the pine tops,
and I pause, panting;
I'm astounded
by such malice
in the Gods;
though this, like beauty,
may be miracle, still
I shall die of it.

And the dogs are closer now
and I break cover again, running
into the rising darkness,
hearing the brute voices behind me
as they track on the stag scent; No,
it is my scent, scent
of my dream and my lust;
and the forest behind me
fills with the terrible potential

of my traitorous dogs;
and the night rises about my legs
like black water.
It is not yet over;
and I pray
in my new soft voice
that I shall waken soon
and find myself man again
and by the pool

where first I saw her.
My breath catches to remember:
How lovely
are the long sinews
of her arm, and her touch of fingers
on the taut bow;
how her beauty fills my throat
with the praise of it,
this song; I spoke

and was revealed.
My heart aches.
I sense a clearing before me,
and I break into it,
through the webbed alders
and the pine thickets,
and the heaving air drowns me,
so full is it of the sounds
of the dogs closing on some poor beast,
and my nostrils flare to catch the last
of my last sunlight,
and as the dogs break from the forest
my fear becomes
this terrible joy,
      for I am caught in the open
searching for her,
Artemis,
      Huntress,
Love of my life.

After Venus,
I loved the Mediterranean

We took breakfast
time after time
in that year
on a brilliant veranda
above the sea.
Morning tea
in white cups
and yellow lemons
on white plates.
And the green sea
was full
of the hollows
of your origin.
    And I tasted salt
in the folds of your body
and in the marrow
of your bones.

I have forgotten you;
and now I taste salt
on bits of broken marble
strewn
along this brilliant
sea blown
coast, salt
on white stone
scattered
like the bones
of a ruined
heart.
You left me only
my tongue, my cypriot,
with which
I now explore
Carthage.

VIII

"I'd like to draw some conclusion from this . . ."

For Jaime, at Home

I'd like to draw some conclusion
from this, but probably won't.

My friend says that daily life
is ultimately unbearable.
He's been hauling out garbage and cutting
firewood long enough to know daily life first hand
and to be entitled to the opinion.
But he's taught himself to bear it;
and though in secret he struggles still,
reserving tuesday and wednesday
for thought, memory, and despair,
the rest of the week, five dailies,
he's domestic. He shares labors with his woman,
helps the sun rise and set, sweeps the day
up into a dustpan, and talks with his friends—
about the mail, his mother's library,
and about the folly of the youth we shared.
He talks of travel now, instead of suicide,

which may be a step toward accepting something.

Taos Spring

In the river
a slender trout
slips free of ice
and glides upstream
to spawn;
and cottonwoods
hover at their year's beginning
in a green haze
of unfolding bud;
and swallows venture out
upon the rising new-warm air;
　　and I, clearing fields,
watch the twisted tap-root
of mesquite, my enemy,
blossom into flame.
And to the east
there's still snow
on the luminous mountain.

Ditch Cleaning

May first,
the last late snow
has come,
catching us outside
cutting sod
along the contours
of the ditch;

       and inside
the close wet cloud
we hear   down valley
the hurry cry
of ducks;
      and they appear
briefly, near us,
         circling,
until finding north
      they disappear
into the whirling
white cloud;

      which lifted
in the night,
and the sun scatters
yesterday's spring snow,
and though the wind is cold still
I sweat,
    breaking
old roots
in this oriental trace
of man-work ditch;

meantime, the warm sun
has come again,
and grass
begins.
      I, too,
have come,
returning home in spring
for the cleaning of the ditch.

The Unborn Father
to the Mother of his Child

Alicia,
the summer's gone and now it's fall
and still you've brought forth
no son or daughter.
Esperate, you say, be patient,
wait till winter.

And so we do,
because we must.
And while we do, I'll tell you
of the fears I have:
I fear that I shall lose you,

for I feel how this unfledged child
takes into itself
your heart; I watch you listen
to what I cannot hear,
and I say goodbye to part of you.

And I fear also
that the mean world to come
will devour this child of ours,
and that there will be for her
more sorrow even than we've had.

And when I fear these things
I wonder if what we've dreamt
and done and said is good.
    And now I'll tell you
of the terrors that I have:

I dream of bannisters
from which I fall;
and I dream also that I am
a gentle and lonely animal,
a kind of minotaur, perhaps,

and that in that self
I am dying,
unable to escape
the coiled perplexity of my dream.
I wake then into the sweat of omens

and I fear
that our child will be born dead,
and I would sit on the ice and rocks,
and I would wail into all the nights
of the year following.

A Moment in Three Lives

Skirl of black birds.
Wind across water
brings pine sound.

My daughter,
six months
into the world,
lies in her basket
in the rushes.
She watches sunlight,
how it moves in the leaves.

My woman's body
is near perfect
in sunlight.
She stoops
at water's edge
and picks
a tiny flower
whose root
is in water.
Her eyes are opaque,
like obsidian;
her heart is deep,
like the pool.
She says little,
yet she knows.

Beginning among rushes,
Voyages.

Dust Devils,
and Other Forms

I was westbound in the truck
toward the ponds, and saw
the dust in standing columns
by O.G.'s dry farm.
Spirits, I think, the aimless
demons of the region
who rise swirling
to reveal themselves
on hot days.

       And earlier
that day, I saw
my infant daughter,
snarled in bed clothes,
nose to feathers, near
smother; and as I turned
her up to air, I saw
the fear disperse,
and the child return.

At the pond, I saw
the mother duck circling
in her shallow world.
Last week there were
three young, this week
there's one. She patrols
the rushes, searching
for the ducklings
that she has, by now, forgotten.

The dust sank back to ground
as the sun set, and
the mother duck took shelter,
and my daughter slept.
And I saw time, in which
we are searching for what
is lost or hidden, and which
consumes both ducks and devils
and everybody's daughter.

For my Daughter,
an Apology

My dead friends promised,
we shall not forget you;
but they too forgot me
as they went away, as they
wandered slowly into the close
dark loneliness of the grave.

But my beloved daughter
child can not forget me,
for I keep returning,
my face appearing
in the darkness above
her crib, my face grave

at times, remembering
that to her I must seem
to die when I go away.
But she too will forget me
when I leave her finally,
when at last I die.

But I promise, my little love,
that I'll betray you less
than I ve been betrayed:
that when I'm alone in death,
I'll remember you,
at least I'll try.

Emergence

For S. Kubrick

These are not words I hear,

it is the woman's rune, the child
song; it is the wave and flux
of mother sound; it is a water
voice, the sleep sound.

And as I listen
the child beast, mine,
wakes with the howling
in its mouth,

and, like a turned tortoise,
flails, reaching for the dripping
star-white nipple.
I change. I am alone.

And I listen now
to the distant jackal
singing to the dead,
and to the desert rustle

of black wings
caressing the dead.
And I hear the hollowness
of the night

fill with the tide of blood
and wailing that rises
in my heart. I turn away
and I hear the far sound

of the stars breaking
in heaven. I turn again,
now toward the other voices,
the voice of the night speaking

with the dog's tongue,
and the wind voice saying,
Tomorrow, go,
into the dry south,

through the salt beds,
down the long descents
through flint
and rubblestone,

tomorrow, go,
into the savannah,
where the beasts live.
And I will;

and the beasts
that I shall kill tomorrow
are saying, *Praise*
the tall grass, the sun

and the least sparrow,
praise the many gods
who have no name;
Praise life,   they say,

and O I would
but there has been no time.
For time is real, and the world
is real, and together, these

give no release
from the toils of brute salvation:
food and shelter, education
of the young, and burial

of the dead. I soon am dead.
I resent the haste; and so
I seek revenge
through some advantage.

I shall invent a thing, this
polished stone:
when in my hand, I will call it
Prayer, and I will use it

to pry loose the jaws
of the black lizard,
to unlock the night,
to untie the knotted heart

of matter. And
with another tool, poem,
not stone,
I shall release my tongue

and speak of my heart's longing
for a better age,
the dream of our first home
by the sea,

the old time
before migration to this dry
and flint hard place. The sea
is a place I do not remember;

but I have heard the mothers
singing to their young,
and the old men singing
to the ancestral dead;

and their songs remember,
and the poem remembers;
and they unlock the dream
that we shall find the sea again,

that we shall bathe in the warm waves,
shall wear the robes of sea grass
and the crown of white shell,
that we shall be what we dream.

But dawn comes. The sun is carried again
out of the distant sea
in the beak of the great slow turtle.
And the dream breaks.

And the child wakes with the game scent
in its belly, and I see
that the child too
shall learn to kill. And I rise

and I follow the scent,
and I run along the fresh trail
holding the prayer tool before me
and singing the prayer to the tool itself

and to death,
and salt tears roll into my mouth,
and I think of my destiny,
which is inescapable,

and of loss, which is real
and perpetual, and of the sea
which I've never seen
nor shall;

and I hear morning voices;
it is our own sweet sunday voices.
We are singing,
Rock of Ages, cleft for me,

I have lost myself in thee.

EPILOGUE

The Fool

That I am ambulatory still
in this age of propulsion,
rage, and mega-yield,
is statistically
astounding;
but I'm a lucky man,
I don't deny it.

And that I create myself
carefully
        with words
amidst so much horror
and confusion
is simply idiotic;

but the cap with bells fits
so I wear it.

Appendix

Easter Sunday, Cordoba

So the summer river bent
its brilliance to our plain,
and beneath the bridges
there was echo even
of the heat,
and sunlight glazed
the flat and tropic stream;
and so we were
in our professions,
through windless days, in heat
and in illumination:
the herdsman kept the mudflats
live with cattle,
and the ferry wove
its senseless pattern
across the ancient loom,
and lines descended
to catch the silver commerce
toward the sea.
But our throats were dry
and we could not sing,
so we made our slow devotions
with hands and cheeks
turned sunward,
and the river was
as molten gold.

1960

ENVOI

Antonio Machado, an austere Spaniard with as good a sense for the soul in language as any, was the first poet I loved. I discovered him nearly twenty years ago. Recently, almost as a ritual evocation of an honored ancestor, I returned again to him and discovered the following: "After truth, there is nothing as lovely as a fiction;"[1] and, of more relevance to what I was about at the moment, this: "Before writing a poem, one must first imagine a poet capable of writing it." I have come to understand this book in that sense, that it contains various and diverse imaginations of myself as Poet. It is the record of efforts across thirteen years in Los Angeles, New York, Spain, Taos and points between, to create myself as something more than Animal with Props (car, gelt, documentation). What I made of myself at first was Man, Animal with Language; and after a time, Man with Voices, Poet. It has been very satisfying, and, from the point of view of saving face existentially, absolutely necessary. Each voice that I have created has attempted to contain and transform some aspect of what was terrible, beautiful, possible or true in certain extreme moments of myself and in certain understandings of the world. But there is (as the reader will discover) manifold coherance here—the obsessions, if you will, of the Author.

The different voices (*personae* or strategies as Pound called them) in this book have emerged out of the elements of feeling, understanding, and place particular to the urgings that made each poem. There are various detached voices (*The Stamp Collection; Crow's Version*); confessional voices, both raw and romantic (*In the Provinces; Magdalene*); voices that speak out of myth or out of history (*Actaeon; The Expulsion; Senator from Carthage*); mannered, sometimes theatrical voices (*Death, Listen; Emergence; Jeremiad*); the voice of the farmer (*Ditch Cleaning; Poem about the Water*); and the voices of my childhood and adolescence (*Childhood I; Childhood II; California Burial*). And there are others. Some are fiction, but none are false.

---

[1] Antonio Machado, *Juan de Mairena: Epigrams, Maxims, Memoranda and Memoirs of an Apocryphal Professor,* translated by Ben Bellitt, University of California Press, Berkeley, 1968.

Looking back, I think that becoming a poet who speaks as many poets was an adaptive strategy. It represents a possible solution to the fearsome character of the world and times we live in: that a self divided can respond selectively (thus more perceptively and with more mastery) to the urgent chaos of stimulae (influences, symptoms, ideologies, needs, facts and prevarications); and that a self not wholly self can respond with some degree of comfortable detachment to the narrowing of hopes and the proliferation of dreadful possibilities. And, furthermore, it is a strategy that reflects accurately the divided aspirations of modern man: whether to realize self or nation or specie, whether to celebrate soul or body—today or on some hypothetical tomorrow. An almost Aristotelian solution to a non-Aristotelian problem. The solution thus depicts the dilemma: that a unified self capable of containing and articulating all stimulae, all truths and facts and the dreams that intercede between them, all selves and worlds, the astounding paradoxes, still eludes. I look forward, however, to such a self, and to the development of a poetic language that will be capable of containing within it all that this book attempts with its many voices.

A few last words: the organization of this book will give no clue, chronological or otherwise, to the nature of the author's *personae*. The organization of the book, in fact, runs against that grain, searching out themes as opposed to selves.

As for aesthetics, the principal idea here has been *Make it Well.* I don't have much use for the Ginsberg dictum of, "first thought, best thought." (Indeed, some of these poems have taken ten years to find out even what they were about.) Also, the poetry here is always intended to be read aloud (*vide* Pound, Olson). Line endings, for instance, are designed to guide the reader to the desired pacing and breathing of the line. And the imagery is primarily aural so that the visual or intellectual image surfaces in the wake of the sound. And the sounds come often, I confess, for their own sake, for the pleasure of them. I have often wished that I could speak Arabic because it is the only language I know that sounds as beautiful as English. But I have always managed to be too busy to learn, what with politics, child rearing, and keeping the weeds out of the garden.

And now as I finish this note and send the final *ms* to the printer, I think that there is hardly a poem in the book that I could not make better. But as Don Antonio goes on to say in the passage earlier, " . . . the poem once written, we can (either) preserve both the poet and his poem; or (we can) disengage the poet and publish his poem." I have chosen to preserve nothing. The poems go into print; the poets who wrote them die. To both I say, go.

Harvey Mudd was born in Los Angeles in 1940, was educated in California and the east, and received a B.A. from the New School for Social Research. He has lived in Spain, served three years in the Army, and worked as a public interest lobbyist. Since 1967 he has lived in New Mexico.

This book is set in Roman on Teton paper.
Designed by Gráfica.

This book is published in an edition of 500 copies, 450 of which are perfect bound, 50 of which are clothbound, signed and numbered by the author.

Santa Fé, New Mexico